CECILIA McDOWALL

VENI, CREATOR SPIRITUS

OXFORD

Commissioned by the Royal College of Organists in memory of Catherine Ennis (1955–2020)

Veni, Creator Spiritus

CECILIA McDOWALL

Gt.: 8', 2', Sw. to Gt.
Sw.: Diapason 8', Principal 4', Reed 8'
Ped.: Principals 16' & 8', Sw. to Ped.

Printed in Great Britain

OXFORD UNIVERSITY PRESS, MUSIC DEPARTMENT, GREAT CLARENDON STREET, OXFORD OX2 6DP

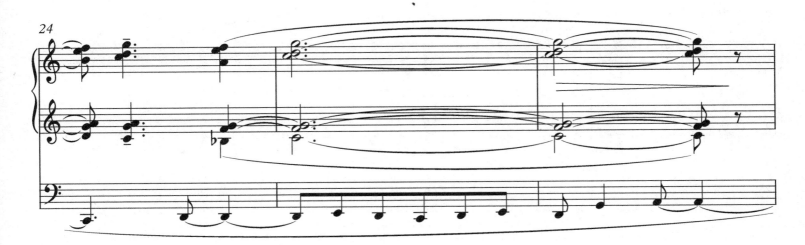

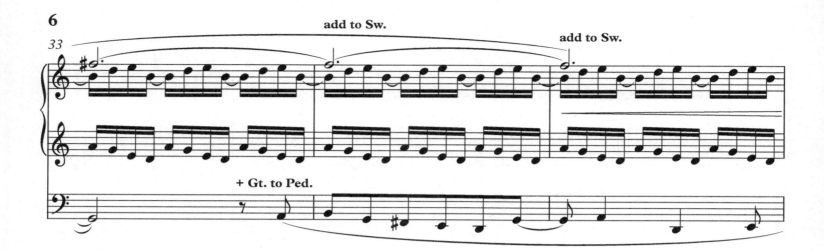